COZY CABIN
COLORING BOOK

**Thank you for choosing Ava Browne Coloring Books.
We strive to publish unique coloring books for all ages.**

This coloring book contains double images, meaning you get to try different colors and shading for every page!!

**If you found this coloring book enjoyable, please leave us a review.
Reviews help drive sales which allows us to make more coloring books.**

This book also includes a free digital copy that you can print out at home. For instructions and your access code, please go to the last page.

**Thank you and happy coloring!
www.avabrowne.com**

Copyright © 2020 Ava Browne Books. All rights reserved. No part of this book may reproduced without written permission from Ava Browne Books.

COLOR TEST PAGE

COLOR TEST PAGE

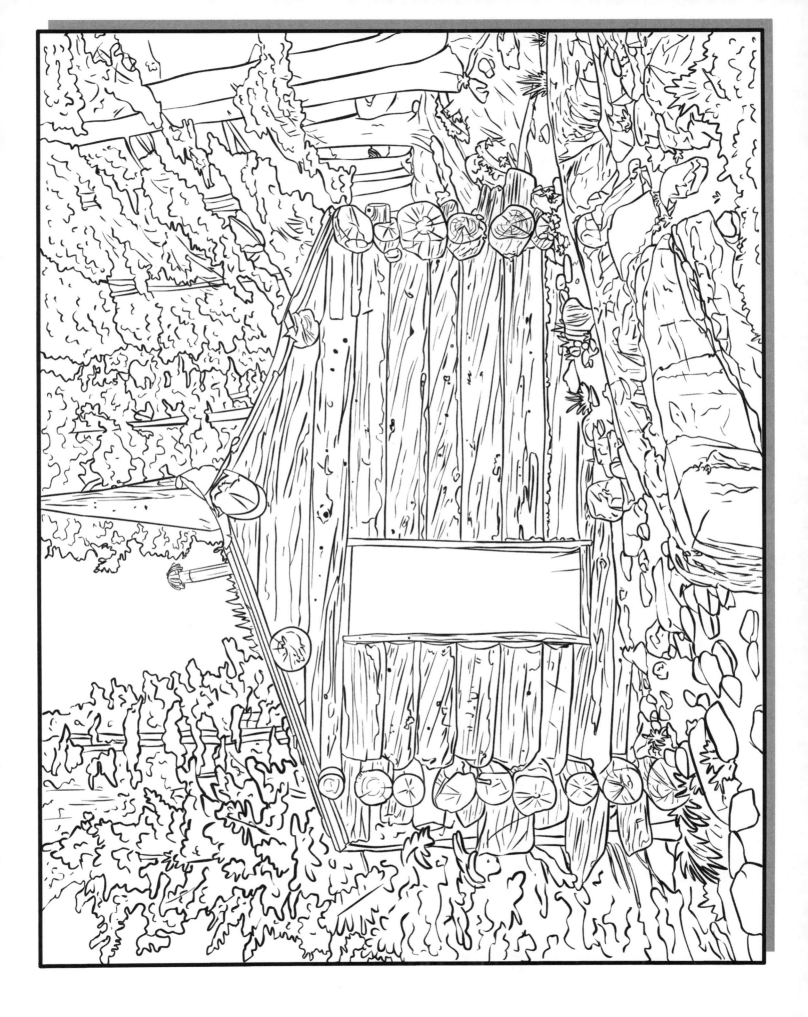

DUPLICATE PAGES START HERE

WE PROVIDE DOUBLE PAGES SO CAN COLOR YOUR FAVORITE IMAGES TWICE USING DIFFERENT TECHNIQUES, SHARE WITH A FRIEND, OR REDO BECAUSE OF A MISTAKE.

DON'T FORGET TO VISIT AVABROWNE.COM TO DOWNLOAD YOUR FREE DIGITAL EDITION WHICH CAN BE PRINTED AND COLORED AS MANY TIMES AS YOU LIKE!

THE DOWNLOAD LINK AND PASSWORD ARE LOCATED ON THE LAST PAGE OF THIS BOOK.

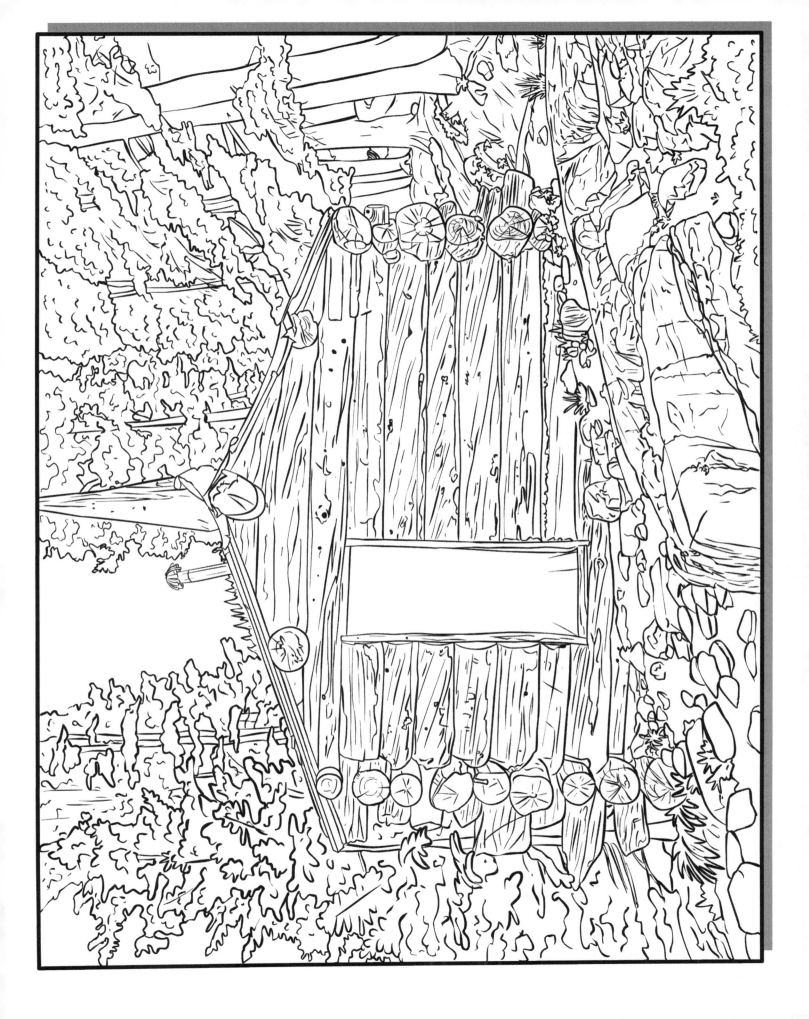

Please visit
https://avabrowne.com/cozy-cabins-download/
to download your free digital copy.

Please consider subscribing to our newsletter, and enter the password xgb9ehu4 to access the file. (All Lowercase)

Printed in Great Britain
by Amazon